Made in Germany

MADE IN GERMANY

Leonard Freed

GROSSMAN PUBLISHERS New York 1970

Photography, text, lay-out: Leonard Freed.
Production: Brigitte and Leonard Freed.
Text lay-out: Jacqueline Schuman.
Cover design: Eberhard Wachsmuth.
Lab-work: Dan Becker and Brigitte Freed.

All rights reserved 1970 by Leonard Freed.
Published by Grossman Publishers, Inc.
44 West 56th Street, New York, N.Y. 10019.
Published simultaneously in Canada by
Fitzhenry and Whiteside, Ltd.
Library of Congress Catalogue Card Number 76-114936
Printed in the Netherlands by
Joh. Enschedé en Zonen, Haarlem.

First Printing

1 Deutschland, Deutschland über alles,
über alles in der Welt,
wenn es stets zu Schutz und Trutze brüderlich
[zusammenhält.
Von der Maas bis an die Memel,
von der Etsch bis an den Belt.
Deutschland, Deutschland über alles,
über alles in der Welt!

2 Deutsche Frauen, deutsche Treue,
deutscher Wein und deutscher Sang
sollen in der Welt behalten
ihren alten schönen Klang;
uns zu edler Tat begeistern
unser ganzes Leben lang.
Deutsche Frauen, deutsche Treue,
deutscher Wein und deutscher Sang!

3 Einigkeit und Recht und Freiheit
für das deutsche Vaterland!
Danach lasst uns alle streben
brüderlich mit Herz und Hand!
Einigkeit und Recht und Freiheit
sind des Glückes Unterpfand.
Blüh' im Glanze dieses Glückes,
blühe, deutsches Vaterland!

Germany will rank first
Always first throughout the world
If the country holds together
Loyally, fraternally.
From the river Meuse to the Memel,
From the Adige to the Belt:
Germany will rank first
Always first throughout the world!

German women, German loyalty,
German wine and German song
Will always stand in high repute
Far and wide throughout the world
And incite us to noble deeds
Till our dying day!
German women, German loyalty,
German wine and German song.

Unity and right and freedom
For the German Fatherland,
For this let us all fraternally
Strive each with heart and hand.
Unity and right and freedom
Are the pledge of happiness.
Bloom in the splendor of this happiness,
Germany, our Fatherland.

In 1952, only the third stanza of the 'Deutschland-Lied,' was proclaimed to be the official anthem of the Federal Republic of Germany.

MADE IN GERMANY... let us retrogress in time and read, MADE IN WEST GERMANY... or still further in time and read, MADE IN THE AMERICAN OCCUPIED ZONE OF GERMANY. One may substitute British, French or Soviet zones for the American.
To know Germany one must remember dates: all discussion, all that has transpired, all statements refer to before or after 1945, 1918, 1933, 1939 and so on. We must remember proclamations: before or after the Währungsreform (money reform) in the Bundesrepublik; the Bodenreform (land reform) in the DDR; the Kulturkampf (culture fight) in the Dritte Reich (Third Reich). German history recalls Luther and his proclamation that lead to the reformation in the church and the ensuing division of allegiance in the principalities between Protestants and Roman Catholics.
Germany has been, in the grips of its history, a divided people: note the German-speaking Swiss, the Austrians. The pivot of Germany's tragedies and its greatest glories has been its geography. All that passes through Europe, east to west or north to south, crosses Germany and has affected its character directly and indirectly.
MADE IN GERMANY means... know your history and geography: Frankfurt am Main is in the Bundesrepublik or West Germany; Frankfurt an der Oder is in the DDR or East Germany. Berlin is the German capital city, but the capital of West Germany is Bonn whereas the capital of East Germany is Pankow. Berlin, controlled by the

four occupying powers, has its 'Berlin Wall' running through and around it . . . stamped MADE IN GERMANY. MADE IN GERMANY at one time meant Silesia, or Pomerania . . . this is now Poland. Centuries in the past, Silesia was marked to Poland . . . a war . . . and it was German; again a war . . . and it is Polish. East Prussia . . . now Russian . . . its main city is no longer Königsberg but Kaliningrad. The eastern frontier of Germany is where? On the Oder river, the frontier of the DDR; the Neisse river, the frontier of the Third Reich; Helmstedt, the last Autobahn stop inside the Bundesrepublik. Germany's allies and friends are . . . the Americans . . . the Russians . . . defending Germany from its enemies . . . defending European civilization . . . defending Germany from itself. The question uncle Moritz asks, 'Will they on the other side,' . . . meaning our uncle Max . . . 'shoot at us?' And I look at uncle Moritz and wonder if he will shoot first at uncle Max.

MADE IN GERMANY means . . . was the Kaiserreich Protestant? Is the Bundesrepublik Roman Catholic? Did the predominantly Roman Catholic west bank of the Rhine river have the right to secede and align itself to Catholic France . . . as some thought right at one time? Does the Roman Catholic hierarchy of the Bundesrepublik want to unite with Protestants of the Deutsche Demokratische Republik? Who should rule Germany? The Rheinlanders, the Bavarians, the Prussians? The socialist? The communist? The capitalist? The national socialist? We think of Germany and think of the three b's: Bach, Beethoven and Brahms or we remember the Brownshirts, Buchenwald and Big Bertha.

MADE IN GERMANY. Why not MADE IN FRIESLAND? Friesland was once a great nation. The Frisian Islands of the North Sea stretch from Denmark to Holland with such poetic names as Sylt, Amrum, Rottumeroog, Schiermonnikoog, Föhr, Pellworm, Wangerooge, Spiekeroog, Langeoog, Norderney, Borkum and Terschelling. Who is to say such names should not be reunited to their former glory as a nation once more? Rubbish, you say . . . at my wedding a bridesmaid recited her poetry in Frisish, published in Frisish for Frisians.

Germany . . . a nation without shape or at best amoebic. Changing its frontier from generation to generation. Alsace Lorraine, has that question at last been settled? What will become of Italy's South Tyrol, where the natives still speak German? Sudetenland . . . an issue settled.

Germany . . . where a friend specially picked and trained to be the future leader of the Thousand Year Reich is now married to a Jewess.

Germany . . .where the first line of a joke begins, 'Wenn das der Führer wüsste' (if this our leader Hitler knew) . . . now over one million Fremdarbeiter (foreign workers) . . . un Aryans . . . from Spain, Italy, Greece, Turkey, the Arab lands and Japan . . . living on German soil . . . loving on German soil . . . making children on German soil.

Germany . . . where the Bundeswehr (West German army) now has black-skinned citizen-soldiers.

Germany . . . where families are now divided between East and West and while they may speak German, they no longer communicate or agree to the meaning of the same words. Nor do they think of the other in appearance or actions as true Germans. The West is Americanized, over-fed, all bosses and pushy with lots of money; in the East they are workers, old-fashioned and Russian. MADE IN GERMANY is a misdemeanor.

Germany . . . the Germany I now speak of is not the geographical, historical Germany of the past, but a segment, a shadow of its former self—now called the Bundesrepublik and the west sector of Berlin. Within this region I have felt free to wander and photograph. The Bundesrepublik is now the richest and most powerful nation of western Europe; a new nation and a new people in search of identity and purpose.

We say MADE IN GERMANY; we mean territorially the East Franconian kingdom of 843.

In twenty-five years from now France will still be France, England will remain England and what can we expect to change in Italy . . . but Germany, what will be of Germany in twenty-five years?

1 Bonn. With my camera I climb over the perspiring human surfaces and view the cavities, the molars. The roar of the voices sounds like the great Niagara Falls pounding the earth's surface. And as man wants to know nature's language, so I want to know this German sea.

2 Berlin. 'It's all the fault of the "Gammler,"' shouted the good people. 'They are un-German. They have corrupted us and we must make war on them,' shouted the newspapers, radio and television. Berlin was their stronghold. With the help of the police and the old people, most of the 'Gammler' were hounded out of the city. Those who were left were thinking of emigrating.

3 Karlsruhe. The fear of a revival of neo-Nazism brought the trade-unionists to the streets in a show of strength. A trade-unionist, an anti-Nazi, extends his hand in greeting to the photographer. How does he know I am not from the police, collecting a dossier for future reference? How do I know he has always been an anti-Nazi? How do we know who is who in this land? Who has been the concentration camp inmate and who the guard?

4 Düsseldorf. The uniforms belong to the local 'Schützenverein' (rifle association), the medals on the breast are toys, the beer bottles are empty and it's all a joke— it's a festival. From out of Rembrandt's night watch they come, pompous and jovial, gluttons for food and drink and always ready to pose for the camera. They are tinkers and tailors and he who shoots the wooden bird down is Schützenkönig (shooting king): he is if he can pay for all the drinks.

5 Hanau am Main. 'From my grandfather,' he said, as I inspected his iron cross. 'It belonged to my grandfather and I have a right to it,' he kept repeating to me. Within societies for the preservation of order, such right is tantamount to the desecration of a hallowed institution. He said his mother gave it to him. 'And what does your father say?' I asked. 'My father is dead. He was killed on the Eastern front.'

6 Etteln, Westfalen. A farming community in a shallow valley. The school, in conventional bureaucratic modern style, was the villager's pride. Affixed to the school wall, on the right as one entered, was the 'Ehrentafel'. It read, 'Honor roll for the dead and veterans of the world war 1914–18, the community of Etteln.' The dead were those within the iron cross; the veterans the others. As I studied the faces closely, some children came up and pointed out their great-uncles, giving me a genealogical history of the village.

3

4

5

6

7 Heiligenberg near Überlingen am Bodensee. Atop the tomb sat a white angel in prayer. There are little tombstones for children in rows here and there. Down over the stones, over the graveyard wall, over the fields, lay the village in a sun-sparkled mist. Under me, the children of the village lay at rest, gazing up to the blue sky, to the motherland. Little white angels in prayer top their stones. The car stops. 'D' or Deutschland, in an oval. I look down at the soldier buried on his back under my feet. Is he still wearing his uniform?

8 Kochelsee. Albrecht Altdorfer (1480–1538), the painter, laid nature bare, humbling man in her mighty power, exposing her terrors and unknowns, divorcing man from reverence of God and himself from her. He drew the great outer fringes of the German forests on scraps of paper, holding them up for man to see. In his drawing of the forest, straight vertical trunks are dark and foreboding, black in the depths where no sunlight penetrates, where no hunter dares enter, where the wild animal is king. Close to the bottom of the drawing, a band of harried hunters darts quickly home through the bush, fear hovering over them for the sun will soon set.

9 München. A river flows through Munich, twisting and gushing its cool aroma over the summered city; it is the Isar. The city's medieval gate is at the river bank. Each day finds the gate and the washing river, ever further from the outer perimeter limits of this growing city.

10 Bergischland. From my notes: the Germans live above the ground and submit to being ruled by a Bundeskanzler and many Oberbürgermeister. These same Germans have a good relationship with another race of little men who live underground, referred to as 'Gartenzwerge' (garden dwarfs). It is a wonder how such a state of affairs continues to exist since the Germans are hard-working practical people, having little truck with children's fantasies. But it does and the German father occupies his time building houses for these people. One need only pass the house of a conscientious German to find his garden cluttered with these little people, well-fed and happy.

11 Hessen. Green nature pushed aside for houses. The colors are bright, white and new, covered with soot. A house and garden of one's own, covering the spreading landscape. The Autobahn connects all in a mad rush around the country.

12 Neuss. At the bank of the Rhine river, a seaman or a riverman sleeps. Sitting at a respectable distance, I studied his tattooed back and took pleasure in his heavy breathing for it created patterns like the wind blowing through tall grass. He groaned, turned his shaved head, and I left him.

13 Hannover. A little old lady in a Konditorei reminisced about afternoon concerts in the public gardens, evening walks and promenades. The city has civil servants, proud and proper people, underpaid in relation to their neat appearances. This is an unhurried town whose major concern is for the welfare of each and every flower. Flowers stand at attention everywhere, on window sills and in public places, all watered and trim. Hannover is a city of show shops and hat shops, of gentlemen sitting in cafes holding white-gloved ladies' hands. A city designed for the lords and the ladies—the capital of Lower Saxony.

14 Hannover. Passing the Autobahn sign which read 'Hannover exit,' we left the farms behind. To the right was the beginning of factories . . . and then we passed a tire factory and the next Autobahn sign said we had passed Hannover and I could see the farmers again.

9 10

15 Castrop Rauxel. 'Thou shalt not kill,'—one of the Ten Commandments from the Bible.

16 Ruhrgebiet. For what is the workingman working? For detergents and soap. The house must smell clean to be clean. Posted signs say 'freshly waxed floors.' Washed clothes receive a coating of black soot if left out overnight. The faces of men become pale and pockmarked, weary and blank, which no amount of soap freshens. Is this for what men are working?

17 Gelsenkirchen. They built this house before the coal mines and the industrial revolution came. Now they are closing down the coal mines and the factories are being built where it is cheaper and the landscape is prettier.

18 Ruhrgebiet. The man is wearing a sign for peace, disarmament, a united Germany, an atomic-free Europe and against fascism.

19 Ruhrgebiet. Down the street come the demonstrators, passing and blending with the landscape like shadows in a haunted house. 'Working men,' they shout, 'remember your champions, your martyrs. Arise ye workers and know your history. It was here on the Wupper river that Friedrich Engels had his factories. It was in Kiel that the navy struck the first note of revolution and the communes were organized in München, that short-lived worker's republic.'

20 Dortmund. This is a city of steel mills, big beer breweries, workers, high wages and hard lives. Through the town, the Easter peace marchers jump and fall, disciplined columns of anti-militarists. From all sides I hear whispered, 'Move only on command.'

16

17

22

23

24

21 Ruhrgebiet. Useless, wasted black mountains creeping from mines outline the homes and children posing in their Sunday best. Perhaps in the future the winds will cover the hills with fertile soil, green trees will grow, they will become parks, and tourists will come as they do to the great Nile pyramids.

22 Westerwald. 'These no-toll highways, with four or more lanes, have no crossings. From these unobstructed roads the beauty of the scenery is unsurpassed.'
... FROM A GOVERNMENT TOURIST GUIDE

23 North Rhine. Sunday excursion to a watering place in the suburbs.

24 Ruhrgebiet. 'As a result of the need to solve agricultural problems and utilize its coal reserves (one of the few natural resources in ample supply), Germany developed as a leader in scientific research.'
... FROM A TEXTBOOK

25 Köln. The Gothic ages gave birth to the cathedral of Köln, an expression of a people's will and effort. Miraculously, American tanks were able to shoot around the cathedral, thus avoiding the complete destruction that befell the vicinity. But even before the war, man in his amicable ways destroyed some of the beauty by building a bridge and train station next to the cathedral.

26 Dortmund. Sunday in the city's park. The family, dressed in tubular, synthetic-fibered suits, walk along the directed paths. Thousands of people are enjoying the water fountains, the park train, the music and cafes. 'So new, so clean, if one only looked in the right direction,' they would remind me, 'one would believe they were still in Dortmund.'

27 Bochum. The fashions reach into the back alleys of working men's homes: now it is to own a poodle of one's own.

28 Mülheim an der Ruhr. An expression common to working young people is 'killing time'; the weekend is spent killing time, waiting for the work days to begin.

29 Köln. None have to beg in Germany, but some do. The police are tolerant when the proper papers show one to be a war veteran with a disability or a disabled seaman.

30 Ruhrgebiet. 'In the old days, a family of six bought eight centners of potatoes for the year, one for each child and two for each adult. Today, they advertise on television for the housewife to reduce and reduce and reduce,' said a housewife.

29

30

31 Leverkusen. World trade inspired Leverkusen, a city factory on a river bank. A chemical factory housing a city population. An industrialist—one man, an individual—said, 'Here it shall be,' and in time grew beyond his wildest dreams. Such men shaped nations, dragging the reluctant along into this twentieth century and making us all modern men, western men, industrial men... machine men. We are products of our society, knowledgeable and respectful of the machine. As the photographer, I am an extension of the camera; I am functional for the film made in the factory on this river bank.

32 Sindelfingen, Baden Württemberg. A programmer in a computer center.

33 Leverkusen. A cleaning girl scrubs the floors in a room sterilized for the production of pharmaceutical products.

34 Böblingen, Baden Württemberg. Twenty-four hours a day, crews take turns at the controls of a computerized machine which produces infinitely complex computer parts for the production of new computer machines.

35 Waldbröhl, Bergischland. A motorcyclist.

36 Siegerland. A motorcyclist couple.

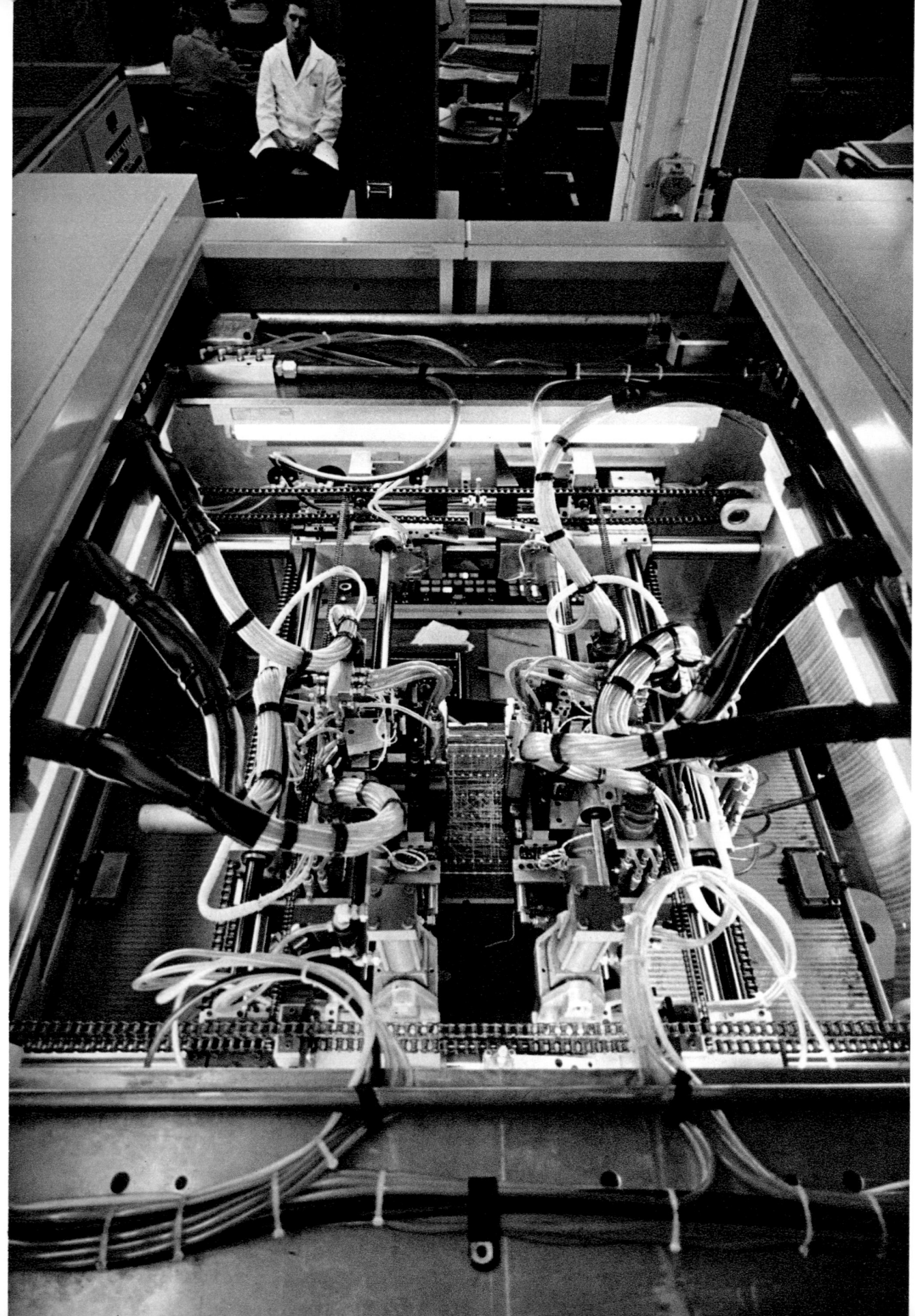

37 Bavaria. Beer-tent.
Drunk we must all be!
Youth is drunkness without wine!
Drink your age again to youth,
This is a wonderful virtue.
For worry worries our lovely life
and the easer of worries is in the wine.

                                          GOETHE

38 Duisburg. Train crews.

39 Düsseldorf. From open beer bottles they drank. Swinging arms around shoulders, clapping, shouting, splattering beer and dribbling; a local shooting club, the butcher, the grocer, the tailor. The cylinder hats were part of the costume, just right for jovial occasions. They pressed me to drink to the full.

40 Hamburg. It is said that until World War II only one hundred or so families owned the city of Hamburg. They owned the land, the banks, the shipyards, the export houses, the industries . . . they owned it; it was theirs—the city hall, the concert hall, the museums, the churches, the hospitals, the police, the firemen, the dogcatchers . . . and they kept it all in the family. They lived together in majestic homes situated along a narrow strip of the Aussenalster, the inland lake of Hamburg just outside the old city walls. I thumbed through the family album in a still private home along the Alsterufer, looking at old photos of the family at play on their lawn that ran down from the house to the Alster Lake, the children and ladies attended by prettified servants. There was a time, I was told, when none in the photos could imagine this scene ever changing, but it did. Hitler, the grandmother knew, was a nasty man and she never feared in the old days to let everyone know her opinion. It seems that Hitler, expressly against her wishes, cut a road through her lakefront lawn, thus permitting the citizens of Hamburg to wander around the Alster at will. It also seems he was out to destroy the power of these families and this was one of his methods. 'If Hitler was a good man,' she said until the day she died, 'he would never have done such a thing to me.'

41 Karlsruhe. Bronze maidens on the fountain; a summer day in the park.

42 Bayreuth. Beethoven's birthplace is Bonn where he looks down from his pedestal in the square, a patron saint of the town. The proximity of Beethoven to the federal government was a fortunate coincidence. What would have happened if Bayreuth had been chosen as the seat of government... with Richard Wagner as its patron saint?

43 Bergischland. A public swimming pool in a park.

44 Freiburg im Breisgau. Mini-canals, one could call them, flowing before the homes from street to street... for children to splash in... giving the city a refreshing natural life and movement of its own.

45 Düsseldorf. The first day of May.

46 Düsseldorf. The first day of May.

47 Bochum. Her son had died at the front and she showed me a yellowing article from the local newspaper describing the action and illustrated with dramatic drawings of the troops heroically defending their positions from overpowering Russian forces... her son had died a hero. On the wall, a framed photograph of herself as a young girl. She can still remember the day she sat with her sister in their new dresses, both anxiously awaiting the photographer.

48 Tegernsee. On the hill, a little cemetery where one may enter and pay homage to the recent dead lying behind a glass partition. The caretaker, in his old German handwriting, has placed a card for those who care: 'eighty-four years of life and a house she possessed.' Between the crosses, a wall separates those native to the village from the newcomers, refugees from the East and retired businessmen; newcomers are buried outside the cemetery. In death, as in life, one's place is fixed; the tombstones are inscribed...handworker, industrialist, faithful servant or housewife and mother.

49 Köln. Church convention.

50 München. The division of Germany deprived Berlin of its surrounding lands and the natural flow of culture that a capital city feeds upon. In time, the unofficial cultural capital gravitated toward Munich, the so-called 'Millionendorf'. Munich is now the fun village, the swinging village, the village for the young.

51 Berlin. Couples in the Tiergarten park. Once this park was the hub of a youthful city, of young couples in love ... now it is memories for the aged in this city of memories and the aged.

52 Koblenz. Wines from the Rhine and Moselle valleys meet here at the Deutsches Eck (German corner). Here are the ruins of old fortresses and castles, here songs and the legends, here the romantic Germany of the tourist guides truly exists. Here all men are Siegfrieds and all women Brunhildes.

53 Westfalen. Flooded cabbage patches.

54 Lippstadt. The rising rivers rampaged through the villages bringing death and destruction. When they subsided, the people came out and cried and laughed and became neighbors.

55 Münsterland. 'Sein Leben war Arbeit,' freely translated, 'his life was work.' The German has the ability to endure stoically natural calamities, to organize for the common good and overcome physical problems.

56 Westfalen. The emergency police move with the grace of a ballet group. Strong muscular young men surround me as they dance. Operatic voices sing commands.

57 Münsterland. Emergency crews free the river from obstructions.

55

56

57

58 Kurhessen. In the valleys the tools of life are made for generations, and the aged and the young function together. It is the asphalt roads hacking through the villages that divide the harmony, which the old still know and the young are forgetting.

59 Oberschwaben. The sun, setting on the Sabbath, brightens the horizon for the morrow. The week's work is done, the fields are at rest and the cows come in from the pasture — the seventh day of the week begins. Throughout the village the streets are being washed and cleaned. From each house the cleaners quietly come to do their work for the Lord; the pastor and the neighbors watch. This is a pleasant ritual to view as one strolls across the countryside and I chat with them and say that I'm staying at the village yonder. Then they say that they've been there and we both look at their road, their village, their sky and together we admire what we see.

60 Weserbergland. For a week I lived in the village. One night I asked about the family down the road and was told only, 'yes, nice people,' so I left it at that. Suddenly the young woman stopped her housework and said, 'but... they are witches, no one dares say it publicly... there is a law; the police forbid it... one can't go around saying such things but it's true... everyone says so... strange things happen over there.' I was warned to keep my wits about me. Another witch was the old woman with the little vegetable garden. Children would become sick after looking into her eyes. Fortunately all the village children knew this and thus avoided her, but it was always a problem with visiting children. The next day I told of seeing gypsies pass and this time she laughed, telling me of the woman who is always running out of her house giving money to the passing gypsies. Some years ago a gypsy cursed her for refusing him money... shortly after that all her cows fell ill; she never forgot it.

61 Oberschwaben. They thought I looked too thin and needed fattening up. Tonight there would be great quantities of beer and they would kill some rabbits, but for the moment we were having potato soup, thick with vegetables from the garden and mouth squares of pig fat and pig feet.

62 Baden-Baden. Between races, the turf of the track is repaired by local people, enabling them to earn some extra money.

63 Oberschwaben. Simple and healthy, without frills, German bread with a little jelly is a meal.

64 Oberschwaben. The woman came from the barn, hammer and sickle in hand. I asked about the tools and she, seemingly for the first time, realized their existence. Then in a great fit of laughter she realized what she had in her hands and crossed the two.

60

61

63 64

65 Stuttgart. The last of the unique acrobatic planes developed during the thirties; the president of the German Aeronautic Club is preparing to take off in it.

66 Kiel. The scars of past history remain, unobtrusive but visible. Above the entrance to a former military institution, the 'Reichsadler' and the Nazi swastika. The swastika, put there in stone before the war, was erased after the war.

67 Darmstadt. There among the many students of the city, the old buildings and bombed buildings . . . where the students lounged, a half-hearted attempt was made to knock off the Nazi swastika.

68 Meersburg am Bodensee. The old castle, the moats, the towers and the polished armor on the wall . . . all as it should be . . . all as we want to remember it.

69 Kiel. The Kieler Yacht Club ball. A framed flag of the yacht club from the 'Kaiserreich 1870'; over the iron cross, the Kaiser crown and the words 'Gott mit uns' (God with us).

70 Ruhrgebiet. I was shown a photo of the grandfather who was wounded in the first world war and his son who was killed in the second world war . . . the family was not proud and told me so.

71 Travemünde, Holstein. Today young men lose their extremities in auto accidents, but as a rule of thumb, those who were of age prior to the second world war, lost their limbs in the war.

72 Karlsruhe. A result of the second world war was that every second German adult male was wounded or killed.

73 Baden-Baden. Are there such things as rules of liabilities and assets affixed to the war loss of limbs? If so, it would seem it works in direct proportion to the individual's economic and social position. The lower the economic and social position, the more the liability; the higher the economic and social position, the more it works as an asset.

74 Meersburg am Bodensee. To explain the above, other factors aside, there is little value in the showing of patriotism for the workingman; a lost arm means the loss of a livelihood. For the upper classes who need not work with their bodies, the wounds forcefully display what need not be said about their patriotism and their right of authority. What are the student corps (die schlagenden Verbindungen) where the students cut each other up but the same manifestation of this principle, a grotesque badge of honor for the privileged few.

75 Kiel. Sailing along the fjords.

76 Köln. The funeral of Dr. Konrad Adenauer, the first Bundeskanzler of the Bundesrepublik.

77 Berlin. The Schlesien territories, lost by Germany and given to Poland after World War II. Millions of refugees left for the West and now meet to renew old friendships, see old loves, speak the old language and hear who died.

78 Bonn. The lawn of the Schaumburg Palast, the office of the Bundeskanzler. The people assemble to pay their last respects to Dr. Adenauer.

79 Bonn. 'Ostdeutschland bleibt deutsch' (East Germany remains German). Sympathizers and former refugees demonstrate in the nation's capital for the return of the lost eastern territories occupied by the Soviets and now administered by Poland.

80 Karlsruhe. June 17, the day of the East German workers' revolt against their government's oppressive measures. In the West this is the day of German unity; students march in torch processions throughout the land.

81 Karlsruhe. 'Auch die Nazis finden wieder ihre Geldgeber,' freely translated, 'also the Nazis find once more the people to help them with money.' A protest is held across from the convention hall where a neo-Nazi party is meeting.

66

67

68

69

71

72

73

74

76

77

79

80

81

83

84

85

82 Karlsruhe. The convention of Germany's neo-Nazi party; the delegates stand after singing the 'Horst Wessel Lied,' the song of the Nazis. Boyish and playful, some delegates wear old Nazi symbols inside their jackets.

83 Bonn. A demonstration for the return of the lost eastern territories; this is the rallying cry of homesick former refugees, the political right wing and the revenger. The banner proclaims, '... und die Steine reden doch deutch,' freely translated, 'in spite of everything, the stones left behind are still speaking the German language.' Other signs say, 'Sudetenland is German land,' 'East Prussia must remain German' and 'the Bonn government supports Israel, not us.'
In a counterdemonstration a small group of theology and philosophy students from the University of Bonn waved banners saying, 'Reconciliation is more important than legal claims,' 'Ask forgiveness, give forgiveness,' and a satirical placard with 'wir fordern: auch Togo bleibt deutsch' (we demand: also Togo – former German African colony – stays German). When I last saw this sign, its holder had received a bloody nose and swollen ear.

84 Bonn. The photographer is of human stature and subject to the realities of a situation. When the photographs do not show what he has seen, it is not the reality but the inadequacy of the photographer and his tools that is to blame.
I have seen the eyes so bulged with hatred, here, between generations that I have understood as never before what it must have been like under Hitler. I have seen how rational beings justify their claim to being a master race as a natural right... how the local butcher can take stick in hand and become the leader of marching Brownshirts, terrorizing a village, a city neighborhood... how they could take men, women and children and burn them... how it all could be natural, justifiable and rational... how all this could happen when the police sympathize with the oppressor and not with the oppressed; when the police and the oppressor become indistinguishable to the oppressed.
What my photos do not show and I must say: that these students (some themselves refugees) have been beaten by this assemblage of parents when asking forgiveness for the crimes of their parents; that the student placard saying 'Niemals vergessen Auschwitz' (Never forget Auschwitz) created the greatest outraged hostility from the parents; that the parents moved on the university grounds while under the protective eyes of the police to beat these students in an attempt to destroy this placard; that certain individual policemen did arrive wearing dark glasses in order to be less identifiable; that these policemen grabbed the placard 'Never forget Auschwitz' from the theology and philosophy students' hands; that these policemen ripped the placard in pieces, demonstrating their authority to settle questions; that these policemen, as a gesture of good will to placate the parents, handed the pieces over to the parents.

85 Bonn. An angry parent reprimanding a university student.

86 Bonn. An angry parent pointing a finger in the direction a student should take—'Rauss aus Deutschland' (out of Germany). With spit, with blows, with words, the parents tell the students that they are shit; that they are not real Germans; that they the parents work and pay taxes so these students can loaf about doing nothing; that they the parents know what is real work; that they the parents would put the students to work, would teach them what work is, in a concentration camp.

87 Gelsenkirchen. Anti-war painting on a truck.

88 Berlin. In the first days after the Wall was erected, American soldiers stood facing East German soldiers backed up by Soviet troops; neither side knew what to do next. By chance I observed the development of an incident within East Berlin. East German police stopped an American officers' automobile for speeding and the officers refused to open their window to any but Soviet officers. From what I learned by listening to the police, they were confused, not knowing why the Americans were creating an incident. It was now a war of nerves between East and West; the Americans threatened to send an army division to retrieve the officers; the East started bringing up their divisions. An anxious world waited hours to know if this was it—war and perhaps the end of mankind. Fortunately the Soviets thought it wiser to speak with the officers and let them go.

89 Berlin. The Wall proved to be extremely effective in its intention—the keeping of East Germans in East Germany. It also proved over the years to be an extremely ugly sight, so sections were removed and rebuilt to make it more attractive. The mine fields, the electric fences, the dogs, the wall, the sharpshooters and towers all remained, but redecorated as parks.

90 Berlin. Children of the West play along this modern medieval wall. To pass from East to West, one goes through a passageway narrower and more complex then many ancient fortress gates.

91 Berlin. Here were the museums, the hotels, the concert halls, and the heart of a city. The Wall is close at hand and a child of the West plays. Among the ruins, a man informs me that the building nearby was once a famous dance hall where he danced.

88

89

90

92 Berlin. Near the Wall is a memorial for one who was killed. Freely translated, 'Heinz Schoeneberger, age 27, from Seesen (Bundesrepublik). On the second Christmasday 1965, at the border gate shot while trying to drive refugees in his automobile across the border to the West. He tried to save himself by running across the border whereupon he bled to death.'

93 Berlin. The Wall under repair. A boy from the West watches.

94 Berlin. A platform has been built for those interested in observing the activities on the other side of the Wall. What does one see? Children and women and old buildings, slow shadows moving. Halfway down the platform a large photo shows people jumping from the building on our left, jumping into this long empty street in the Western sector. Along the Wall a sign is posted, 'Strassensperrung verursacht durch die Schandmauer' (street closed as a result of this scandalous wall). In a little park nearby stands a stone monument, 'Den Opfern des Nationalsozialismus' (for those killed under the national socialist); a small stone next to this one reads, 'Errichtet aus Steinen der durch Rassenwahn verwüsteten Synagoge Fasanenstrasse' (built from the stones of the synagogue destroyed because of racial hatred); nearby another stone, 'Den Opfern des Stalinismus' (for those killed because of Stalinism). After this I walked to the university grounds. Outside a student building, this large and pleading notice was on the bulletin board: 'handelt christlich an ihnen... Afrikanischer Student sucht Zimmer' (be a good Christian to an African student looking for a room).

95 Berlin. An American soldier eats his lunch during a crisis along the Wall.

96 Dortmund. Before the first world war the old man was a famous writer, but now he is forgotten, a footnote in German literature. He said, 'I've had many libraries. Some were given away by me, some were taken away from me. When I was young it mattered. I was a revolutionary but I thought such things were permanent; books were like bricks, to be built into the house of literature. Where can one find my early books today? Nowhere, all destroyed.' He spoke of Bismarck—how he as a little boy had sat upon his father's shoulders as the statesman went by and how he and the crowd waved to the glorious and prosperous future ahead.

97 Köln. 'Pray,' she says to the little girl, 'pray and you shall go to heaven.'

98 Baden-Baden. The race tracks.

99 Kiel. Professors marching in a line. A little old lady professor in the line is being honored. 'Who is she?' I ask. 'She is Frau professor, a very famous Frau professor from America,' I was told. 'But why have they invited her?' 'To honor her, after all she is one of us; she was born in Germany . . . but she was a Jewess and emigrated.'

100 Frankfurt am Main. The outside of the Paulus church. Here, in the year 1848, the professors and doctors convened to create a democratic Germany. It was the German states shining moment and opportunity, but the liberal-revolutionary professors and doctors talked and talked until at last many had to flee to America.

101 Hannover. Strollers in the public gardens of the palace peep through the window.

102 Hannover. If one is permitted to peep, then all should be permitted to peep.

103 Hannover. Reception inside Schloss Herrenhausen.

104 Brühl, Nord Rheinland. The waiters prepared for a reception inside the Augustusburg castle. 'I should photograph them because of their handsome qualities,' they said. 'What qualities?' I repeated after them. 'Their leg qualities,' they said and went in to serve their distinguished guests.

105 Hannover. The government composed a book on etiquette for those entering the government service. It remains best remembered for one bit of advice known as the ceremony of the toilet. It describes how castles and palaces being what they are or even homes for that matter . . . places where ladies and gentlemen come in close contact and where it is often required for minutes at a time for the sexes to excuse themselves. Thus the rule: to avoid the irritating sounds emanating from the body and to avoid disclosure to those guests within hearing distance . . . flush the toilet and keep it flushing.

106 Hannover. When the ruling class on social occasions are among their equals and individually shed of their protective subordinates, the camera takes on a power of its own to shatter the vanities of man.

107 Baden-Baden. The gambling casino.

108 München. It is difficult not to notice it:
Fritz no longer savors Sauerkraut.
Fritz no longer dresses in Lederhosen.
Fritz no longer wears boots and
no longer clicks his heels.
Fritz likes neither the old Kaiser
nor any other Kaiser.
Fritz is really no longer named Fritz.
And he does no longer say: 'Jawohl!'
    . . . FROM AN ADVERTISING SUPPLEMENT SPONSORED AND PREPARED BY THE PRESS AND INFORMATION OFFICE OF THE FEDERAL REPUBLIC OF GERMANY.

109 Kiel. The yacht basin.

110 Kiel. Round and round we sailed. He said that he did not care for sailing but it was useful for him to be in the club. His customers were always impressed when he gave them permission to pull at the sails.

111 Lübeck. The banks of the Trave river.

101

102

108

109

TRAUMA I

'... I can see only one means by which the end can be attained, and that is to arouse an energy of national pride, so real that it becomes a second nature to repel involuntarily everything which is foreign to the Germanic nature. This principle must be carried into everything; it must apply to our visits to the theater and to the music-hall as much as to the reading of the newspapers. Whenever he finds his life sullied by the filth of Judaism, the German must turn from it and learn to speak boldly about it. The party of compromise must bear the blame for any unsavoury wave of anti-Semitism which may arise.'

...FROM LECTURES ON POLITICS.
HEINRICH VON TREITSCHKE (1834-1896)
PROFESSOR OF HISTORY AT THE UNIVERSITY
OF BERLIN

TRAUMA II

I wandered through the camp; it was for the unemployable or little employable; the barracks were left over from the war.
The camp's director said he had studied economics in his youth but being the father of eleven children, had learned to accept his lowly position in society. 'One has to be stern or there is no order,' he repeated, telling how once one of his sons objected to his measures and ran out to join the youngest of the Hitler youth groups known as the 'pimpfs'. Then, having signed up, he returned to his father saying that now that he was in the party, the party would protect him ... whereupon the father immediately beat him. 'One must understand the party officials,' the father said to me. 'Here in Schleswig-Holstein they are more understanding of the good old traditions then in other parts of Germany.' Having lived through both world wars he found that in many ways the Nazis did good. 'Their economic policy was good; for example, if one didn't want to work, he would be put into a work camp. That was good, but

some of the other things weren't. The Gestapo, that was bad and I even told the wife of the police chief so... I wasn't afraid and nothing happened to me. With the Jews, that wasn't right... the smashing of store windows, I told them it wasn't right and nothing happened to me. I told it to them this way. All the food you destroy and smash really belongs to the people. Why do you destroy the goods of the Jews; better to give it to the people... yes, I have it in writing that I left the S.A. in 1935... I could see something was bad. Now, I say the Nazis did lots of good but sometimes they went too far... the breaking of Jewish store windows was bad, the times were bad, people were hungry, they had no work or money... now, the Jews really helped the poor.' 'How?' I asked him. 'I'll tell you how. The Jews were willing to sell cheaply and live on fifty Pfennig a day while the others needed at least five or six Marks a day to live... so if the Jew could manage to live on what he earned, well that was good for the poor. Germany should stop giving money to other countries and first help its own people. The present government is not interested in the poor. Good Nazi economics is what is needed in this camp to get some of these asocial people to work instead of spending time making children... some should be sterilized.'

TRAUMA III
In the rooms of the camp it was dark, damp and greasy. A woman was peeling potatoes and there seemed to be children all over. At the window a woman said her son had been killed fighting in the French Foreign Legion; he was an adventurer. The son's father, a Dutchman, had been brought to Germany during the war to work in the slave labor factories. Her family name was now Jerusalem... 'like the city in Egypt.' Her present husband told her he had trouble in Adolf's time... they thought he was Jewish (she couldn't stop laughing at that). 'But,' she said, 'he was no Jew. There were lots of people in the town with that name.' After a while she said to me so that others shouldn't hear, 'I don't go along with these crazy ideas, to me all people are people—black, white, Jews.' Does she have problems with the name today? 'No, at Christmas time people think it is a fine name. One of the neighbors is called Morgenstern (morning star) and all the neighbors toast to the Morgensterns over Jerusalem.'

TRAUMA IV
I drove on and let him talk. He was a student going home to Lübeck for the weekend; he was hitchhiking but next week they would deliver his new car. He expected in twenty years to be at least a school director in some small town. He had tried the army and had spent two years as an officer, but as a career it had possibilities only for the higher officers and sergeants.

Then he spoke of the Wall in Berlin. The problem was the Americans; they weren't hard enough, not really ready to fight. The East German guards along the Wall were all thoroughly indoctrinated against the West and this, he seemed to imply, was good reason to shoot back. The West Germans were weak, not having enough national pride... where, he wanted to know, was Germany's pride in being once the nation of thinkers and poets, equaled only by the ancient Greeks.

As we neared Lübeck he began speaking boldly, 'I must say what I think. The German people have given much too much money to the Jews and Israel... it is only our government that thinks it has not done enough. We Germans want to be friendly with all races; now it's time to help the Egyptians... one can't talk too much because here in Germany it's such a hot subject, but other countries also wanted to get rid of their Jews... only the Germans had the courage to do so. The Jews have only themselves to blame. Now that the Jews have their own country, why don't they all go there and leave us alone.'

He left and I thought... keep faith, one must not abandon those Germans still fighting to uphold democratic ideals... German democracy is still too fragile to survive without outside support.

112

113

115

116

117

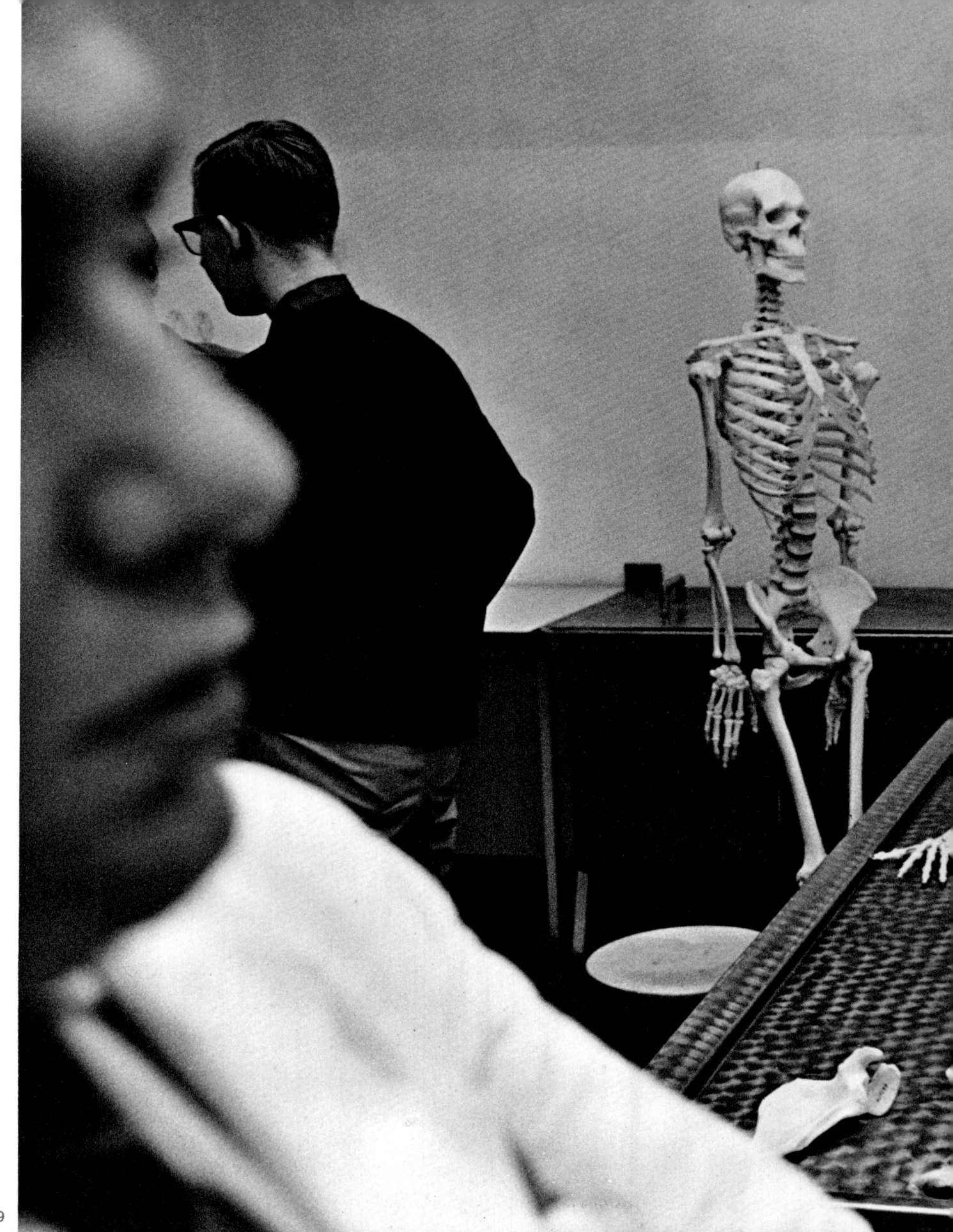

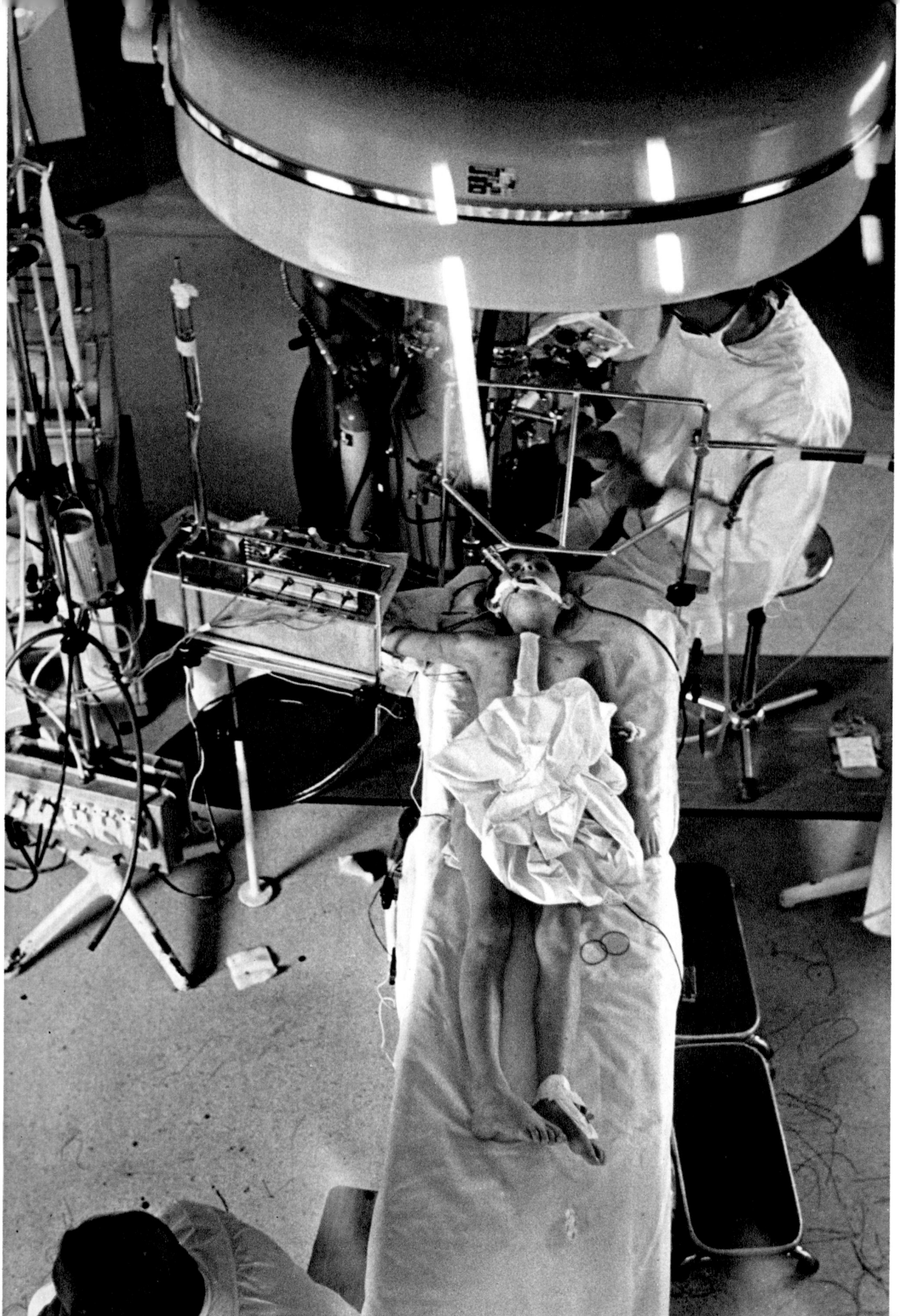

112 Kiel. Children shake their parents' hands before going to bed. There is the story of the little boy who cried when his mother would say, 'Give your nice hand to the people,'—the right hand is the nice hand. He wanted to know what was wrong with his other hand.

113 Köln. Poor they came, rich they return. Turkish workers going home for the summer holiday after a year on the job and a year from their families; laden with transistors, new suits, bicycles . . . going home means making another baby before returning to the northland.

114 Landshut, Bavaria. In 1474, a great princely wedding took place here in what is now a small provincial town. Be not fooled; when Berlin was a village, Landshut celebrated its wedding. Such is the joyous rememberance of the population that they keep repeating the whole affair.

115 Bayreuth. We walk through the palace in wonder and after taking the grand tour, we still marvel at the genius of man to create new palaces in faraway places.

116 Köln. Across the frontiers it rains . . . in Amsterdam . . . in Paris . . . in Köln.

117 Köln. 'Jedermann' (everyman) is a German stage play depicting man's existence between birth and death.

118 Hamburg. To feed the industrial needs of a nation, complex harbors are built up over more and more land.

119 Düsseldorf. University medical students in an anatomy class. The staggering complexity of modern industrial society is best illustrated in man's scientific study of man. Perhaps the ultimate will be the complete reassembling of industrial man.

120 Düsseldorf. Completion of an open-heart operation on a young girl.

121

122

121 Düsseldorf. An architect's family.

122 Oberkassel. An artist's family.

123 Frankfurt am Main. The book fair.

124 Bayreuth. The public garden.

for Rose and Sam